FR. SLAVKO BARBARIC, O.F.M.

THE WAY OF THE CROSS

In accordance with the decree of Pope Urban VIII and Act II of the Vatican Council, the writer states that he does not wish to question church authority to which he submits completely. The words "Apparitions, messages, miracles" and others have, in this book, the value of human testimony.

ISBN 0-940535-29-7
Published by: Parish Office
88266 Medugorje

FR. SLAVKO BARBARIC, O.F.M.

THE WAY OF THE CROSS

With Jesus and Mary
from Golgotha to the Resurrection

Presenting the artistic
work of
CARMELO PUZZOLO

MEDUGORJE

Dear Faithful!

In this booklet you will find the comfort you need whenever you desire to be near Jesus, who suffered for us, and near Mary, who as Mother, suffered much with Him, and continued to suffer after His death until the Resurrection.

For us who are travelers and are surrounded by daily sufferings, confronted with our personal, family and world sufferings, it is good and redemptive to be near Jesus and Mary. They show us how we can walk towards a new life and how every cross and every torment can be transformed into the resurrection.

The passages from Holy Scripture and Our Lady's messages, as well as the short meditations, all are intended to help you enter into the mystery of suffering and gain the assurance that you are not alone. Just as Our Lady remained with Jesus until the last moment, she and her Son will not abandon you.

We will help you enter into Jesus' and Our Lady's suffering, not only with Scripture and Our Lady's messages, but also with the Stations of the Cross, Jesus' way of the cross. The images were sculptured with much love by Carmelo Puzzolo. His experience of Our Lady's presence in Medugorje inspired him to make her image present in every station. In order for you to understand and discover the artist's idea more profoundly, we present in this booklet his description of every station of the cross.

Therefore, if you are praying in front of each station on Krizevac, before your prayer, in silence, observe momentarily the people around you.

If you are praying alone at home, for one moment have a mental image of family and friends. The pictures of the Stations of the Cross in the booklet will help you make the Way of the Cross.

By handing this booklet over to you, I desire that you come closer to the suffering Savior and His suffering Mother, who helped Him to redeem the world. Since they are always close to one another, let us call this Way of the Cross: WITH JESUS AND MARY, ON THE ROAD TO GOLGHOTA AND THE RESURRECTION.

Let us all be vessels filled with God's blessings, the blessings of love and peace. We especially wish this for Carmelo Puzzolo and his family, and the families who have donated the sculptured art work for the Stations of the Cross.

*   *   *

Before we center in on prayer, let us remember that praying and meditating on the passion of Christ, and the sufferings of his Mother, means to allow:

- *That the love manifested by Jesus' sufferings touches our sufferings and changes them into love.*

- *That the trust Jesus had in his Passion transforms our lack of trust into new hope.*

- *That the unity of Mary and Jesus in their sufferings, heals all our wounds and our divisions.*

- *That the divine forgiveness given by Jesus at the moment of his death, touches our hearts and opens them so we can forgive and also be reconciled.*

- *That the cry from the Man-God on the cross stirs up profoundly in the depths of our being, goodness and love.*

- *That our sufferings are united with the sufferings of humanity.*

- *That the bitterness experienced by Jesus, transforms all our bitterness into the joy of fulfilling the Father's will.*

- *That the death of the Man-God on the cross transforms our death into the new life of the resurrection.*

- *That the fidelity demonstrated by Mary in her sufferings heals us of our infidelity.*

- *That the courage of Jesus frees us from our timidity.*

- *That human evil manifests itself as the reply to divine Goodness and admonishes us not to leave space for evil in our lives.*

- *That the rage and hatred of mankind remind us not to give space to our passions.*

Meditating on the Passion of Christ and the suffering of Mary, means to make possible the meeting of the human and the divine, and the glorification of the divine in the renewal of the human.

Therefore it is important to:

- *take time, because haste does not permit you to meet the person who is suffering;*

- *take time, because our wounds will not be healed hastily;*

- *take time, so as not to run the risk of passing by someone who is suffering without understanding.*

If you can not find enough time to take some of the suggestions that are proposed to you here and allow the strong message to go into the depths of your heart, desire from this meeting with Jesus' and Mary's sufferings, that you may feel yourselves renewed, with a heart full of peace, ready to love and forgive, healed in spirit and body.

Jesus, you are alone in the Garden of Gethsemani.

Jesus is in the Garden of Gethsemani.

He is alone, even if He seems to be surrounded by His disciples. Begging them, Jesus had told them: "Stay here and watch with me" (Mt 26:38).

Perhaps, in His humanity, He had hoped for comfort from His disciples until the last moment; at least from those three whom He wanted close to Himself; but, as God He knew that these men could not have soothed His anguish.

In such a cruel moment, only His Holy Mother could understand His pain. Only Mary, enlightened by the Holy Spirit and faithfully keeping all the teachings of her Son in her heart, could have comforted Him.

Only His Most Holy Mother, with her presence, her loving and adoring silence, with her sensitive and immense goodness, could have tempered the bitterness of such a despairing anguish.

Jesus did not want Mary with Him, because with His mother at His side, Gethsemani would not have been the place of supreme detachment, the climax of the redemptive and coredemptive offering of the Passion. There was no comfort whatsoever for Jesus, who was annihilated in pain and loneliness. Through prayer, He surrenders to the Father's Will: "Father, may Thy will be done." The "fiat" of Jesus is received by the Father.

The angel who comes down from heaven is the visible message, the symbol and the instrument of the Father's mercy which helps Him. "An angel from heaven appeared to him to comfort him" (Lk 22:43).

"Then, after singing songs of praise, they walked out to the Mount of Olives. Jesus then said to them, "Tonight your faith in me will be shaken, for Scripture has it: I will strike the shepherd and the sheep of the flock will be dispersed " (Mt 26:30).

Then Jesus went with them to a place called Gethsemani. He said to his disciples, 'Stay here while I go over there and pray.' He took along Peter and Zebedee's two sons, and began to experience sorrow and distress. Then he said to them, 'My heart is nearly broken with sorrow. Remain here and stay awake with me.' He advanced a little and fell prostrate in prayer. 'My Father, if it is possible, let this cup pass me by. Still, let it be as you would have it, not as I.' When he returned to his disciples, he found them asleep. He said to Peter, 'So you could not stay awake with me for even an hour? Be on guard, and pray that you may not undergo the test. The spirit is willing but nature is weak.' Withdrawing a second time, he began to pray: 'My Father, if this cannot pass me by without my drinking it, your will be done!' Once more on his return, he found them asleep; they could not keep their eyes open. He left them again, withdrew somewhat, and began to pray a third time, saying the same words as before. Finally he returned to his disciples and said to them: 'Sleep on now. Enjoy your rest! The hour is on us when the Son of Man is to be handed over to the power of evil men' (Mt 26:31, 36-45).

We adore you O Christ and we bless you because by Your Holy cross you have redeemed the world.

Jesus, now I want to remain in silence, and in my heart I repeat your words: "Father, may Thy will be done."

Spend some minutes in silence. You are advised to stay in silence as long as possible, repeating the same words for yourself and for others, including the sick whom you know.

Jesus, I do not want my heart to sleep anymore. Here I am, I present myself and I am with you...

Mary, you were not in the Garden of Gethsemani, but you were not sleeping in that hour. You were present with your motherly love, in spite of the physical distance. Help me now to walk with you and your Son, because I want to be with you .

INTRODUCTORY PRAYER

Jesus and Mary, I am walking with you now, following You, Mother and Son, on the Way of the Cross. In this way, I desire to show you my love and devotion. I confess that on many occasions I was not only far from you while you were suffering but I also have caused the heavy blows you received by my words and actions, and inflicted wounds in your hearts, just as I, in the same way, have inflicted wounds in the hearts of my brothers and sisters.

Every time I was selfish, proud, insulting, untruthful; when I enjoyed myself at other people's expense; or when I did not offer what I had to others, I inflicted you with wounds, Jesus and Mary, because everyone of us is your brother, your sister, your son, your child. Jesus and Mary, I repent for all the evil I have committed, so that I will be able to follow you and share in your sufferings.

Accept me. Unite me with your pain, so I can, by my own wounds and sufferings, contribute not only to my personal salvation, but to the salvation of mankind.

By your example Jesus and Mary, I accept my way of the cross, my family's way of the cross, my community's, my Church's and the world's way of the cross. I want to be part of the redemption of the world with you, to participate in its salvation.

Have mercy on us, O Lord!
Have mercy on us!

O Mary, Mother of Sorrows,
Intercede for us.

At the Cross her station keeping,
Stood the mournful Mother weeping,
Close to Jesus to the last.

Holy Mother, pierce me through,
In my heart each wound renew,
Of my Savior crucified.

Jesus, you are condemned to death

Jesus is between the soldiers and Pilate. Below are the enraged mob. They want Jesus crucified. People, angry, influenced by the chief priests, are shouting and threatening with their fists and with sticks raised. The soldiers and the people are awaiting Pilate's verdict, who after a fearful attempt to save the Man, washed his hands and handed Him over to His killers.

The hurt pride and vanity of the Scribes and Pharisees are changing to, "Crucify Him." Among the fists and sticks which were raised in a sea of hatefulness, the Christ, who in spite of His disfigured body resulting from the many beatings, still shows His majestic grace. He directs His gentle, sad look towards those who condemn Him, and penetrates their hard-shelled hearts. From His swollen face, forgiveness is sensed for the whole of ungrateful mankind.

The only comfort to Jesus is the presence of His Mother. Her presence is discreet, but real; their hearts blending into one pain.

From the Bible: Yet I, like a trusting lamb led to slaughter, had not realized that they were hatching plots against me: "Let us destroy the tree in its vigor; let us cut him off from the land of the living, so that his name will be spoken no more."

(Jer 11:19)

- We adore you, O Christ, and we praise you.
- Because by your holy cross you have redeemed the world.

My Jesus, you were judged, but you never judged. Therefore, what Pilate said is true: "Here is the Man." It is a terrible moment for you and your Mother Mary, to be just and innocent, and in return to be severely treated by people who wounded your heart and the heart of your Mother, uniting them into one heart of suffering and pain. After a lifetime of freeing the innocent and protecting the rejected, you were made equal not only to the rejected, but also to the outlaws. O, how it must have increased your pain.

Jesus, forgive us for what we have done to you. Jesus, forgive us for continuing to do the same whenever the innocent are killed, the just are judged and whenever the poor are not helped.

Jesus, I promise now that I will lower my fists and lay down my stick, which I have raised so many times on those around me. I also pray for those who are afraid to protect the innocent, the righteous poor and the ill.

Message: Dear Children! This evening in a special way I am calling you to perseverance in trials. Ponder how the Almighty is still suffering today because of your sins. So when sufferings come, offer them as a sacrifice to God. Thank you for having responded to my call.

(29 March 1984)

- We thank you, O Mary, and we bless you.
- Because by your sufferings you helped to redeem the world.

O Mary, I want to be with you here. You are alone and the world has joined its forces to destroy your Son.

You are not retreating even though you are helpless. You knew, as a Mother, how important it was to be near your Son in those most difficult moments. Here I am, Mary. I am accompanying you, so that you will not be alone among people who hate, reject, condemn and seek death.

I am joining you with my love, my compassion, my readiness to be near those for whom your Son and you suffer.

Have mercy on us, O Lord!
Have mercy on us!

O Mary, Mother of Sorrows,
Intercede for us.

Through her heart, His sorrow sharing,
All His bitter anguish bearing
Now at length the sword had passed.

Holy Mother, pierce me through,
In my heart each wound renew,
Of my Savior crucified.

Jesus, you are taking the heavy cross on your already wounded shoulders

The big heavy cross appears as if it needs to be balanced on Jesus' shoulders. People who are following Him, are still holding the cross, but are prepared to let this sad procession begin. There are some who are hurrying them on with curses and threats. Some are bowing before Him, mocking and trying to provoke Him. But He is gentle and keeps silent, leaning on the wood of the cross with the crown of thorns on His head. He is ready to take His first step to Calvary. As in the previous station, Mary is there in the right corner of the scene.

From the Bible: Jesus was led away, and carrying the cross by himself, went out to what is called the Place of the Skull (in Hebrew, Golgotha).

(Jn 19:17)

- We adore you, O Christ, and we praise you.
- Because by your holy cross you have redeemed the world.

Jesus, it is truly sad that you had to experience so much suffering from us. You are in pain. Your strength is diminishing, and on your back is a heavy wooden cross. While the cross was being put on your shoulders you experienced curses, blasphemy, mockery and heavy blows. And you, like the sacrificial Lamb, did not resist.

O my Jesus, I desire to offer to you a comforting word. Your Mother has not deserted you. She cares and is following you on the way. Although she cannot take the cross on her shoulders, she accepted it and took it into her heart and shared your burden. Therefore, in full confidence I can say that you Mary, took the cross on your motherly shoulders, and into your motherly heart.

In front of this scene, with my eyes full of tears, O Jesus, the sufferer and the Mother, the sufferer, I am heartily sorry for my behavior towards you. I am heartily sorry that, because of my behavior, I have placed crosses on my shoulders and on the shoulders of people around me.

Jesus, I promise to change my life and my behavior. From this moment on, I would prefer that others lay crosses on my shoulders than I ever lay my cross on theirs.

I promise to intercede for those who carry crosses and will try my very best to prevent these scenes of the Crucifixion from ever happening again. Forgive me Jesus, for not preventing evil in situations where I was able to. From now on, I will be near those who suffer. I accept my limitations to help, but will not distance myself. I am ready to suffer silently like your Mother did.

Message: Dear Children! During these days while you are joyfully celebrating the cross, I desire that your cross also would be a joy for you. Especially, dear children, pray that you are able to accept illness and suffering with love, the way Jesus accepted them. Only in that way, will I be able to give you the graces and healing which Jesus allows me. Thank you for having responded to my call!

(11 September 1986)

- We thank you, O Mary, and we bless you.
- Because by your sufferings you helped to redeem the world.

Mary, I seriously want to remain with you. I want to learn from you how to suffer with others even when I cannot help them. And to you Mother, from the depths of my heart, I thank you for the painful walk, alone with your Son. Amen!

Have mercy on us, O Lord!
Have mercy on us!

O Mary, Mother of Sorrows,
Intercede for us.

Oh, how sad and sore distressed
Was that Mother highly blessed
Of the sole begotten One!

Holy Mother, pierce me through,
In my heart each wound renew,
Of my Savior crucified.

Jesus, you fall for the first time under the cross

The weight of the cross is terrible. After only a few steps Jesus falls. He has already suffered so much. The unmerciful beatings have weakened Him. The road is steep and difficult. Jesus tries to push himself up with His elbows. It appears as if He wants to use this fall to rest a little, but He is being pulled by His robes to continue walking. Mary's suffering is more apparent. Her Son becomes the bridge between the Father and the people by the cross He is carrying.

From the Bible: Therefore I am content with the weakness, with mistreatment, with distress, with persecutions and difficulties for the sake of Christ; for when I am powerless, it is then that I am strong.

(2 Cor 12:10)

- We adore you, O Christ, and we praise you.
- Because by your holy cross you have redeemed the world.

Jesus, as I see you falling, I am aware that you are not completely on the ground. You remain in that position as a bridge, the bond between man and the Father, a bridge that will overcome all obstacles reconciling all who are divided, and healing all who are wounded. You are the High Priest, the builder of a new road leading us to that union with the Father. Thank you for accepting the cross. Through it you opened a new road for me.

O Jesus, High Priest, I pray for all who follow you, answering your call. May they be like you Jesus, ready to sacrifice everything, ready to be a victim for the salvation of mankind.

Jesus, with Mary I pray for my parish priest, for all chaplains, for all priests, especially those who are tired and heavily burdened, those who are not faithful to you, those who have failed, and those leaving the priesthood. I also offer my prayers for Bishops and for the Pope, and for those who are prevented from spreading the "Good News", who are being persecuted because of your Name. May they know the joy of suffering in love with you.

Give grace to your priests so that they may be able to raise in confessions all those who have fallen. May all priests be your image. Amen.

Jesus and Mary, here I also give you my life. All that I have and all that I am, I am uniting with you. I pray to you for love, that love with which you accepted pain. I desire to have it in my heart too. Give me love in my heart so that my heart will be devout, strong and not proud.

Message: Dear Children! Today I am calling you to the love which is loyal and pleasing to God. Little children, love bears everything that is bitter and difficult for the sake of Jesus, who is love. Therefore, dear children, pray to God to come to your aid, not however according to your desires, but according to His love. Surrender yourselves to God so that He may heal you, console you and forgive everything inside you which is a hindrance on the way of love. In this way, God can mold your life and you will grow in love. Dear children, glorify God  with the canticle of love so that God's love may be able to grow in you day by day to its fullness. Thank you for having responded to my call.

(25 June 1988)

- We thank you, O Mary, and we bless you.
- Because by your sufferings you helped to redeem the world.

O Mary, I cannot understand the immense pain you suffered because my heart does not love as your heart does. I cannot comprehend the depth of your love, how you desire to bring all people close to your motherly heart, and how it pained your soul to be so helpless and only witness the suffering of your Son.

Have mercy on us, O Lord!
Have mercy on us!

O Mary, Mother of Sorrows,
Intercede for us.

Is there one who would not weep
'Whelmed in miseries so deep Christ's
dear Mother to behold?

Holy Mother, pierce me through,
In my heart each wound renew,
Of my Savior crucified.

Jesus, you meet your grieved mother

A station dedicated to all mothers and pilgrims! We again see the big cross that dominates the scene. Jesus and Mary's closeness becomes a meeting. The weight of the cross almost disappears into a natural suspension, consenting to a last embrace. Mary gently caresses the face of her suffering Son. Jesus responds in an affectionate way. This is a moment of profound suffering and tender emotion. We understand how a woman bows in respect while those who are without feelings are trying to prevent this moment by hitting and pulling Jesus. I personally wish that each pilgrim and every Christian would experience exactly this in their sufferings, that Mary's closeness would become a meeting which comforts and consoles.

From the Bible: See, my servant shall prosper, he shall be raised high and greatly exalted. Even as many were amazed at him—so marred was his look beyond that of a man, and his appearance beyond that of mortals...

(Is 52:13-14)

He grew up like a sapling before him, like a shoot from the parched earth; There was in him no stately bearing to make us look at him, nor appearance that would attract us to him.

(Is 53:2)

- We adore you, O Christ, and we praise you.
- Because by your holy cross you have redeemed the world.

Jesus, in all your pain, you were comforted when your eyes met your Mother's eyes. She was following you alone. Her closeness is now a real meeting. She did not try to remove the cross from your shoulders, her presence is encouraging for you.

O Mary, this moment was possible because of your devotion, and you neither ran away from suffering, nor were you afraid of your Son's suffering.

Thank you for comforting Him with your gentle hand, giving Him strength within. Thank you Jesus, for responding with gentleness to your Mother. You knew how much she was suffering.

Jesus and Mary, thank you for walking together through suffering.

Jesus, now with Mary, I pray for all mothers and fathers who are suffering, because of their children. I pray for those who cannot meet again, because they are prevented by human injustice and condemnation. I also pray for all those who do not want to meet each other again, because there is no more love and no trust in their hearts.

Message: Dear Children! Today I am calling you to complete surrender to God. Everything you do and everything you possess give over to God so that He can take control of your life as King of all you possess. That way, through me, God can lead you into the depths of the spiritual life. Little children, do not be afraid because I am with you even when you think there is no way out and that Satan is in control. I am bringing peace to you. I am your Mother and the Queen of Peace. I am blessing you with the blessing of joy so that for you God may be everything in life. Thank you for having responded to my call.

(25 July 1988)

- We thank you, O Mary, and we bless you.
- Because by your sufferings you helped to redeem the world.

Mother Mary, caress with your gentle hand all those who are looking for you, and all those who are not, because it is so sad to be without a mother. Ask for all mothers to be faithful to their motherhood. Embrace all of us. Renew us and your church, because the church is looking at you, as the star which guides us to the final salvation.

Have mercy on us, O Lord!
Have mercy on us!

O Mary, Mother of Sorrows,
Intercede for us.

Can the human heart refrain
From partaking in her pain,
In that Mother's pain untold?

Holy Mother, pierce me through,
In my heart each wound renew,
Of my Savior crucified.

Jesus, Simon of Cyrene is helping you carry the cross

Jesus is at the center of the scene. His strength is gone. He seems to be drawn to the ground by His own weight. He looks as if His muscles no longer exist. His head is tilted to His left with fatigue and it is held up compassionately by one of the men from the crowd. The Cyrenian powerfully proceeds forward, but also shows his compassion towards the Nazarene. This compassion is that of those who still believe in Jesus. The other part of humanity is visually absent, but is present and is symbolized by the falling shoulder, deformed by the cross and the ugly mocking sign hanging around Jesus' neck.

In the background we see the isolated pain of Mary.

From the Bible: He summoned the crowd with his disciples and said to them: "If a man wishes to come after me, he must deny his very self, take up his cross, and follow in my steps." Finally, when they had finished making a fool of him, they stripped him of the cloak, dressed him in his own clothes, and led him off to crucifixion. On their way out they met a Cyrenian named Simon. This man they pressed into service to carry the cross.

(Mk 8:34, Mt 27:31-32)

- We adore you, O Christ, and we praise you.
- Because by your holy cross you have redeemed the world.

Jesus, the meeting with your mother strengthened you and comforted you internally. That is why they gave you Simon of Cyrene, to carry the cross for you. He was strong, and he carried the cross willingly. His help is of great benefit for your journey of obedience to your Father.

You assured your disciples that they would not be asked more than their own strength. But even when our strength leaves us, we always find someone, like Simon of Cyrene, who will help us to continue our journey. Thank you Jesus, that from the example of Simon of Cyrene, I can learn that even my role is important. Even my spiritual strength, my intellectual and physical strength, could be a guarantee for someone, that he won't be asked more than his own strength. That is why, with sincerity, I will now put everything that I have and all I am at the disposal of those who suffer.

O Jesus, accept me! May my hands extend and help those who are no longer able to work with their own hands. May my eyes give light to those who cannot see. May my feet give help to those who are not able to walk. May my word give voice to the dumb.

Here I am; take me into your service.

I am sorry that many times I have not realized where I could be useful, or that I have not been ready to help, because I was seduced by my own selfishness. Forgive me, Father. Often, many people have been left behind, or have fallen into temptation, because of my idleness in putting to good use my gifts.

Message: Dear Children! God wants to make you holy. Therefore, through me He is inviting you to complete surrender. Let holy Mass be your very life. Understand that the church is God's palace, the place in which I gather you and want to show you the way to God. Come and pray! Neither look to others nor slander them, but rather let your life be a testimony on the way of holiness. Churches deserve respect and are set apart as holy because God, who became man, dwells in them day and night. Therefore, little children, believe and pray that your Father increase your faith, and ask for whatever you need. I am with you and I rejoice because of your conversion and I am protecting you with my motherly mantle. Thank you for having responded to my call.

(25 April 1988)

- We thank you, O Mary, and we bless you.
- Because by your sufferings you helped to redeem the world.

O Mary, make it so that even when I have to be apart from those who suffer, my existence will be a sign that I love them and that I do not want to abandon them.

I pray especially, O Mary, for those who care for the gravely ill and who must look helplessly on, like you at this moment, at the pain and anguish of their loved ones.

Let love grow in everyone and make them available to serve others.

Have mercy on us, O Lord!
Have mercy on us!

O Mary, Mother of Sorrows,
Intercede for us.

Bruised, derided, cursed, defiled,   Holy Mother, pierce me through,
She beheld her tender Child,   In my heart each wound renew,
All with bloody scourges rent.   Of my Savior crucified.

Jesus, Veronica is offering You a cloth to wipe your face.

Veronica leaves a group of women to go to Jesus. He turns towards her so she can wipe His face. The pity of the women on the left, amongst them Mary, who share their maternal feeling with those of Veronica, contrasts with the scorn of those who, deaf to every feeling, use whips and sticks to impede and brutalize the tender, affectionate, and brave gesture of Veronica. Among the shouts and the offensive attitudes, instinctively there is someone who tries to hold up the cross, perhaps to make less painful this brief rest.

From the Bible: Who is this that comes from Edom, in crimsoned garments, from Bozrah-- This one arrayed in majesty, marching in the greatness of his strength? "It is I, I who announce vindication, I who am mighty to save." Why is your apparel red and your garments like those of the wine presser? "The wine press I have trodden alone, and of my people there was no one with me. I trod them in my anger, and trampled them down in my wrath; their blood spurted on my

garments; all my apparel I stained. For the day of vengeance was in my heart, my year for redeeming was at hand."

(Is 63:1-4)

- We adore you, O Christ, and we praise you.
- Because by your holy cross you have redeemed the world.

Jesus, with gratitude and love you lowered your face so that Veronica, in her love and gratitude, could wipe it. And for you, O Mother of Sorrows, it was a comfort to see and know that there were still people who wanted to help and show their love towards your Son when you were prevented from doing so. You were observing this gesture with much gratitude.

Mary, I know that you were particularly thankful to the brave Veronica. Therefore, your pain was united with hers. Jesus, I pray for the sick and suffering, that they may accept with gratitude, all the help and love they receive from those who are caring for them. Grant patience to all who are sick, and to those who are nursing them. Help all who are close to the sick, so that in them they may see and experience you. Particularly, I pray for all who have lost their strength through the illness of their close ones. May they renew their love for you in every glass of water they offer to the sick.

I pray for all hospital staffs, doctors and nurses so that they, with love, will serve you and your sick brothers and sisters. May those who assist never be on their own. May you educate, Jesus, through your Mother Mary, the hearts of those who love the sick and the suffering, and with their love redeem their pain.

Jesus, I pray for all confessors, who, with the strength of your grace, are at the service of the reconciliation of men with the Father. Please help everyone to remember that the power is in your hands. After every confession let the priest experience the same happiness felt by Veronica. Let those who go to confession receive with joy the grace of reconciliation and of purification.

Message: Dear Children! From day to day I wish to clothe you in holiness, goodness, obedience, and the love of God, so that from day to day you can be more beautiful and better prepared for your Lord. Dear children, listen to my messages and live them. I desire to lead you. Thank you for having responded to my call.

(24 October 1985)

- We thank you, O Mary, and we bless you.
- Because by your sufferings you helped to redeem the world.

Even you, Mother of Sorrows, found comfort when you realized that there was still someone who was prepared to give help and proof of love to your Son, as you were unable to do it. I wonder with what kindness you would have accompanied Veronica's human gesture.

I give you thanks, O Mary, because with your love you will be able to help those who, even today through those who suffer, seek to serve your Son with love. Amen.

Have mercy on us, O Lord!
Have mercy on us!

O Mary, Mother of Sorrows,
Intercede for us.

For the sins of His own nation
Saw Him hang in desolation
Till His spirit forth He sent.

Holy Mother, pierce me through,
In my heart each wound renew,
Of my Savior crucified.

Jesus, you fall the second time under the cross

An increased violence prevails in this dramatic scene. Jesus is seen again with His knees on the ground, His hands and His blood are in the dust. It seems He wants to embrace the rocks on the ground. Again the crowd that followed is over Him shouting and threatening. Someone holds the cross. Others bend down to pull His hair. Others show fists and sticks. Some observe in silence. Hands frantically try to lift Him to put Him under the weight of the cross. Again, on the right, we see Mary's face in anguish.

From the Bible: But Zion said, "The Lord has forsaken me; my Lord has forgotten me." Can a mother forget her infant, be without tenderness for the child of her womb? Even should she forget, I will never forget you. Kings shall be your foster fathers, their princesses your nurses; bowing to the ground, they shall worship you and lick the dust at your feet. Then you shall know that I am the Lord, and those who hope in me shall never be disappointed.

(Is 49:14,15,23)

- We adore you, O Christ, and we praise you.
- Because by your holy cross you have redeemed the world.

Jesus, you fall again, drained of your strength. You are weighed down by the cross and cannot form a bridge. You are closer to the ground, embracing the rocks which are softer than the hearts of the people who are torturing you, hitting you, pulling your hair, and violently pushing you beneath the cross. Your Mother is in deep anguish over your pain.

Jesus, I am ashamed to say this to you: thank you for all the suffering you accepted for us. It is becoming too much. The people's hatred is still not satisfied. Thank you even more for getting up and showing us that you are prepared to love until the very end.

Jesus, I pray for all those who are disappointed with themselves, who fell into sin again, who were overwhelmed by hatred, who surrendered to blasphemy, who were misled by selfishness, although they had made a commitment to correct themselves. I also pray for those who have tried to get out of drugs and other sinful slavery, and then fell again, instead of walking straight forward. They found themselves beneath their crosses and are crawling on the floor humiliated by sin and therefore rejected by people.

Jesus, grant that none of your brothers and sisters who have fallen yet again, remain crushed and broken. Help them to get up yourself, Lord. You understand them even when others do not, and you accept them when others are rejecting them. You will not pull their hair, like yours was pulled, at that fall.

You will find ways and the time to help them, without inflicting new wounds, reopening old ones.

Thank You Jesus, because You do this through the intercession of your Mother, who is troubled in heart from pain.

Message: Dear Children! I am calling you to love your neighbor. Love those from whom evil comes to you. In that way you, with love, will be able to discern the intention of hearts. Pray and love, dear children! With love you can do even that which you think is impossible. Thank you for having responded to my call.

(7 November 1985)

- We thank you, O Mary, and we bless you.
- Because by your sufferings you helped to redeem the world.

O Mary, thank you that through your suffering you have learned to obey like your Son. You want to be Mother and Auxiliatrix of all. Thank you, because it has never been known that you refused help to anyone who turned to you for help. Amen.

Have mercy on us, O Lord!
Have mercy on us!

O sweet Mother! fount of love,
Touch my spirit from above,
Make my heart with yours acco

O Mary, Mother of Sorrows,
Intercede for us.

Holy Mother, pierce me through,
In my heart each wound renew,
Of my Savior crucified.

Jesus, you are consoling the tearful women of Jerusalem

As Jesus climbs Calvary, He meets a group of women from Jerusalem. Filled with pity from the scene, they cry and beat their breasts. Jesus stops to speak to them: "Do not weep over me, but weep for yourselves and your children."

Between Jesus and the women there is a reciprocal pity. Christ's compassion extends to all humanity whose sins are the real cause of all ills and of His sacrifice. Meanwhile, within the group, hate prevails, and violence is expressed by furious acts.

Even in this situation, Jesus finds the strength to console others. A frightened child seeks refuge with his mother.

From the Bible: On that day I will seek the destruction of all nations that come against Jerusalem. I will pour out on the house of David and on the inhabitants of Jerusalem a spirit of grace and petition; and they shall look on him whom they have thrust through, and they shall mourn for him as one mourns for an only son, and they shall grieve over him as one grieves over a firstborn.

(Zec 12:9-10)

- We adore you, O Christ, and we praise you.
- Because by your holy cross you have redeemed the world.

Jesus, you are a teacher, and you use every occasion to teach and to preach. You are a prophet and in every situation You proclaim God's word.

Thank You Jesus for every word you announced, proclaiming salvation, love, peace, mercy and forgiveness.

Jesus, I pray for myself first. Give me the grace to hear your word on every occasion in my life. Help me so that I will never miss any, and that I will be lead by your word as your Mother was. Forgive me for all the words that I have taken so lightly. Purify me and free me from the guilt which comes from disobedience to your word.

I also pray for all those who are spreading your word, for all those responsible in the world and the Church. May they be primarily the listeners and executors of your word, so that they can spread the same to others with the power of your Holy Spirit. I pray for all teachers and professors, for all responsible for the upbringing of children, especially parents.

Jesus, make the hearts of all educators similar to yours, and make productive what they do. Purify the hearts of parents and educators. Help them to be less selfish so that in their humility and simplicity they can fulfill the marvelous mission of enlightening and educating others.

Jesus, cure us from spiritual deafness so that every word from you will touch us profoundly.

Message: Dear Children! You do not know how to love and you do not know how to listen with love to the words I am saying to you. Be aware, my little ones, that I am your Mother, and that I have come on earth to teach you how to listen out of love, and how to pray out of love and not compelled by the fact that you are carrying a cross. Through the cross God is glorified in every person. Thank you for having responded to my call.

(29 November 1984)

- We thank you, O Mary, and we bless you.
- Because by your sufferings you helped to redeem the world.

O Mary, in this station your face is not hidden. But I know that you are near your Jesus, and that you listened with love to what He was saying to the women, because you have always been a faithful listener and executrix of the word of our Lord. Join, Mary, to your pain and grief, those who are suffering because they do not listen to the words of your Son, teacher and prophet of humanity.

Have mercy on us, O Lord!
Have mercy on us!

O Mary, Mother of Sorrows,
Intercede for us.

Let me share with you His pain,
Who for all our sins was slain,
Who for me in torments died.

Holy Mother, pierce me through,
In my heart each wound renew,
Of my Savior crucified.

Jesus, you fall for the third time under the cross

This third fall is dominated by the overturned cross that is nearly hidden. It is dimly seen among the men that try to hold it. Its weight for a brief moment does not lie heavy on our Lord's shoulders. Everyone is crowding around Jesus, whose body can be seen through the legs of the crowd that pushes, curious to see.

Jesus' hands are groping wildly in the dust. His face is nearly touching the stones and it seems that He wants to kiss that piece of earth, a witness to the last steps of His earthly reality.

Jesus' body is reduced to a heap of rags. They try to lift Him up, but He is exhausted, crushed by the weight of his sufferings. The Virgin seems wrapped in her grief. Some women share her pain. Truly it is nearing the moment predicted by old Simeon, "A sword will pierce your soul." Never had our Savior been seen like this, the Man of pain, despised, trampled, rejected by mankind. He suffered and didn't say a word, like a Lamb that lets itself be taken to be slaughtered.

From the Bible: Come, all you who pass by the way, look and see whether there is any suffering like my suffering, which has been dealt me when the Lord afflicted me on the day of his blazing wrath. From on high he sent fire down into my very frame; He spread a net for my feet, and overthrew me. He left me desolate, in pain all the day. Give heed to my groaning; there is no one to console me. All my enemies rejoice at my misfortune; it is you who have wrought it. Bring on the day you have proclaimed, that they may be even as I. Let all their evil come before you; deal with them as you have dealt with me for all my sins; my groans are many, and I am sick at heart.

(Lam 1:12-13,21,22)

- We adore you, O Christ, and we praise you.
- Because by your holy cross you have redeemed the world.

Jesus, I am breathless at this sight in front of me. I sympathize with you and your Mother, and my Mother. I would like to see more people who are willing to help you, and accept you, but they are not there. You are abandoned in your pain, falling to the ground. Mary is by your side. She is near, but another meeting is not possible. You are meeting the rock and embracing it. O Jesus, Man of suffering, sacrificial lamb who has, in this way, taken away the sins of the world, and who has purified the earth which is stained with all kinds of crimes, we thank You for your innocent sacrifice, offered out of love for us.

Jesus, I pray now for all those who feel thrown to the ground by life's circumstances, and for all those feel crushed and destroyed by pain. I pray for those who do not know to whom to turn to anymore, for those who never meet a human face and helping hand, but only see stones, dust and mud raining down upon them. Particularly I think of those who are psychologically ill, and are therefore rejected by their families and the hospitals. Sickness has stripped them of their identity.

I also pray for those who confide in fortunetellers or are victims of witchcraft, for those who give themselves to occult practices and magic, and who have therefore fallen under evil influence. Free them, so that they may follow the light. Help them find their way out of darkness.

Jesus, with the power of your fall, free all those whom Satan has taken under influence and is trying to destroy in body and soul. Lamb of God, sacrificed for us, deliver us from all evil.

Message: Dear Children! Today I want to tell you that God wants to send you some trials which you can overcome with prayer. God is testing you through the trials of everyday. Pray now that you may overcome every temptation peacefully. Through every trial that God tests you with, come to Him more open, and approach Him with love. Thank you for having responded to my call.

(22 August 1985)

- We thank you, O Mary, and we bless you.
- Because by your sufferings you helped to redeem the world.

O Mary, thank you for consenting to be the Mother of the Messiah, the Savior; Mother of Him who accepted a walk so great and who endured such suffering.

O Mary, Mother of Sorrows, be near those who help others who are losing themselves. Help them!

Have mercy on us, O Lord!   Mix'd with yours let my tears be,
Have mercy on us!   Mourning Him Who mourned for me,
   All the days that I may live.

O Mary, Mother of Sorrows,   Holy Mother, pierce me through,
Intercede for us.   In my heart each wound renew,
   Of my Savior crucified.

Jesus, they strip you of your clothes

Jesus has arrived at the place of the execution and the soldiers are stripping him. In spite of the atrocious suffering and the physical exhaustion, He is still able to stand up and He does this with majestic royalty.

This is the moment, before the nails penetrate Him, that the face of Christ shows all the suffering, the pain of the physical beating and, even more, the anguished offense to His spirit, to Him who is Creator and Redeemer of humanity. But never, as now, are His divine virtues so evident in His face.

At this moment the fury of the men seems to subside. Even if someone tries to provoke Him again, Jesus looks at humanity with love and compassion.

He wants from us an act of repentance, and He is ready to save us. The Mother is comforted by a woman friend.

From the Bible: Farewell, my children, farewell: I am left desolate. I have taken off the garment of peace, have put on sackcloth for my prayer of supplication, and while I live I will cry out to the Eternal God. Fear not, my children; call upon God, who will deliver you from oppression at enemy hands.

(Bar 4:19-21)

- We adore you, O Christ, and we praise you.
- Because by your holy cross you have redeemed the world.

All has been created by you, O Jesus, because you are the Word of the Father, and now you have to endure such humiliation!

The men have done everything possible to destroy you, but in spite of that, you stand upright with majestic royalty and show that you have remained "man," a real man, and we can repeat Pilate's words, "Behold the man!"

My Jesus, while observing you in this scene, I remember only one word, turn us into human beings once again because we have become inhuman. Families have become inhuman, communities and the whole of humanity have become inhuman. That is the reason why so many have been deprived of their material well being and die of hunger. They can hardly go on. But the number of those who are deprived of their spiritual well being is even higher. Therefore they are totally blocked in their human path and they are in danger to become completely dehumanized. Many don't know Christian and human virtues anymore because they have completely distanced themselves from positive values, inflicting evil to their soul, spirit and body. Oh Jesus, please make people more human.

I pray to you, Jesus, for those who, as a result of abusing their body, have become sick in their spirit and in their body, and have contracted incurable diseases.

By virtue of your sacrifice, Jesus keep away from the young and new generations every dubious attitude that would infect their bodies and their spirits.

For the wounds that made you weak, without diminishing your dignity, please make humanity follow a dignified path.

Message: Dear Children! Today I call you to open yourselves more to God so that He can work through you. The more you open yourselves to Him, the more you will receive the fruits from it. I wish to call you again to prayer. Thank you for having responded to my call!

(6 March 1986)

- We thank you, O Mary, and we bless you.
- Because by your sufferings you helped to redeem the world.

Mary, intercede for those who at this moment are exposed to their passions and save them from ruin.

Have mercy on us, O Lord!
Have mercy on us!

O Mary, Mother of Sorrows,
Intercede for us.

By the Cross with you to stay,
There with you to weep and pray,
Is all I ask of you to give.

Holy Mother, pierce me through,
In my heart each wound renew,
Of my Savior crucified.

Jesus, they are nailing you to the cross

Everything is still, everything is silent. The vibrant blows of the hammer set the scene. Even the guards have finally quieted and help silently. Three robust executioners nail Jesus on the cross. Jesus doesn't move. He doesn't cry. From His mouth, dry from the fever, not a word is uttered.

His behavior would be enough to show those present that an innocent man was being condemned. To the contrary, their hearts are already anticipating the long awaited victory over "The Rabbi of Nazareth," and they don't know — and can't even imagine — that He is praying for them and is predisposing His spirit to the extreme sacrifice. Mary is immersed in deep pain that is wrapped around her like a cloak.

From the Bible: Though he was harshly treated, he submitted and opened not his mouth; like a lamb led to the slaughter or a sheep before the shearers, he was silent and opened not his mouth. Oppressed and condemned, he was taken away, and who would have thought any more of his destiny? He was cut off from the land of the living, and smitten for the sin of his people.

(Is 53:7-8)

- We adore you, O Christ, and we praise you.
- Because by your holy cross you have redeemed the world.

In front of the scene of the crucifixion, even your enemies, O Jesus, remain, for at least a moment, in silence. The echo of the blows from the hammer, together with the physical pain you are experiencing, is an icy spectacle. Even your mother is touched by the pain. It is a moment in which neither can console the other.

(Silence)

O Jesus, at this moment I want to express, once more, my gratitude for all that you wanted to accept and bear for us. I desire your pain to have a profound echo in my heart and to touch within me all that still remains obstinate, mean and insensitive. By your pain create a new heart within me. May the blows endured by your hands open those hands that have been transformed into fists. May your pierced feet stop the way of those who have chosen the wrong path. May they guide them back onto the right path. May your pain, O Jesus, touch every harshness within the family, in the Church and in the world.

Message: Dear Children! I would like to thank you for all the sacrifices and I invite you to the greatest sacrifice, the sacrifice of love. Without love you are not able to accept either me or my Son. Without love you cannot pass on your experiences to others. Therefore, I invite you, dear children, to begin to live love within yourselves. Thank you for having responded to my call.

(27 March 1986)

- We thank you, O Mary, and we bless you.
- Because by your sufferings you helped to redeem the world.

O Mary, through your abundant suffering, make it so that the world will stop being ruthless and that there will no longer be people who are pained, alone and abandoned. May, a new world be born. O Mary, through your pain and that of your Son. May new souls and hearts be born ready to suffer for love, and so redeem a world not yet redeemed. Only love, fed by your love, can become a balsam to the wounds we have inflicted on one another and because of which we have suffered much. May, O Mary, the church of which you are the model and the Mother, and of which your Son is the head, become a community of people who love one another closely, that it may soften and redeem the world. I entrust to you particularly the sufferings produced from hate, from the longing of domination over others, from envy, from selfishness and from infidelity. May those who suffer for love always be fortified by love itself, so that they will not tire, nor stop, but will be generous and persevering witnesses of that love which redeems and saves.

Have mercy on us, O Lord!
Have mercy on us!

O Mary, Mother of Sorrows,
Intercede for us.

Virgin of all virgins blest!
Listen to my fond request:
Let me share that grief of yours.

Holy Mother, pierce me through,
In my heart each wound renew,
Of my Savior crucified.

Jesus, you are dying on the cross, immersed in atrocious pain

The horizon is broken by the three crosses, and Christ is raised vertically in the center. Jesus, after having entrusted the Mother to the son and the son to the Mother, turned to the Father who is in heaven and said, "Father, forgive them because they know not what they do." These are holy words that on their own are enough to give hope to the hearts of men. After a last deep breath, Jesus dies. The sky grows dark, the earth shakes, there is fear and terror. Most run away, lost and immersed in their own anguish. Mary kneels down, embraces the cross and kisses the crossed feet of her Christ in an extreme show of love. John, the faithful, tries to comfort her, without taking his eyes off the beloved Master. Below, wrapped in their cloaks, Mary Magdalen and Mary of Cleofa are crying.

From the Bible: My God, my God, why have you forsaken me, far from my prayer, from the words of my cry? I am like water poured out; all my bones are racked. My heart has become like wax melting away within my bosom. My throat is dried up like baked clay, my tongue cleaves to my jaws; to the dust of death you have brought me down. Indeed, many dogs surround me, a pack of evildoers closes in upon me: they have pierced my hands and my feet; I can count all my bones. They look on and gloat over me.

(Psalm 22:1,15-18)

- We adore you, O Christ, and we praise you.
- Because by your holy cross you have redeemed the world.

For three hours, O Jesus, you hung on the cross. For three whole hours, O Mary, you suffered incredible pain with Him. Each breath of His on the cross, every movement of His face, every word of His and especially His last cry are driven like swords into your heart, already prostrate from the pain. O Jesus, Savior, even with your great suffering, you never forgot your Mother. You didn't even forget your disciples. You entrusted them, one to the other. You did not forget those who whipped and crucified you. For them, you invoked pardon.

You do not die in the bitterness of hatred, but you clothed your tremendous passion with forgiveness and with love.

Thank you, Jesus, that in your way you opened up a new road to humanity: the road of peace and of love. So, I pray to you now, along with your Mother Mary, Queen of Peace and our Mother, to give your peace to the world. By your passion and her intercession, may the heart of every injured person be renewed. Let the river of reconciliation, of which you are the source, run within each person. May your injured heart, from which gushed blood and water, purify my heart and the hearts of all men from all spiritual sickness. Your blood eliminates all pain and creates new meaning to the growth of love, so that the world will be saved.

Message: Dear Children! In these days I want to invite you to put the cross at the center of everything. Pray especially in front of the cross, from which great graces are coming. In these days, make a special consecration to the cross in your homes. Promise not to offend Jesus nor the cross and promise not to bring about insults to them. Thank you for having responded to my call.

(12 September 1985)

- We thank you, O Mary, and we bless you.
- Because by your sufferings you helped to redeem the world.

O Jesus, I accept with joy Mary as my Mother, because I know that through John you have given her to me also. O Mary, I thank you because you accepted me freely as your child, as you freely accepted John. Let a new communion with you surge in my heart at this awesome, saving moment. Thank you, because many people faced with this scene have thrown away their poisoned swords and arrows, their whips and sticks of sin and have undertaken a new life with you.

Have mercy on us, O Lord!
Have mercy on us!

O Mary, Mother of Sorrows,
Intercede for us.

Let me, to my latest breath,
In my body bear the death
Of that dying Son of yours.

Holy Mother, pierce me through,
In my heart each wound renew,
Of my Savior crucified.

Jesus, they take you down from the cross and entrust you to your Mother

Mary cannot bear this laborious descent from the cross, her pain makes her faint. The crowd that assisted at the death of Jesus has disappeared. The few faithful to the Master have remained and are intent on accomplishing the compassionate act of recovering the lifeless body of Jesus. The death of "The Rabbi" caused a great delusion for those who did not have deep faith. Only the Mother and a few close ones remained under the cross. Even the apostles have nearly all gone. Meanwhile, for the hard of heart, the nightmare of that Man is finished. With His doctrine, He disrupted their existence and tormented their hearts. Jesus was lowered carefully, until His tormented body had no longer to undergo other injuries. The disciples support the Mother of Sorrows.

From the Bible: Since it was the Preparation Day the Jews did not want to have the bodies left on the cross during the sabbath, for that sabbath was a solemn feast day. They asked Pilate that the legs be broken and the bodies be taken away. Accordingly, the soldiers came and broke the legs of the men crucified with Jesus, first of the one, then of the other. When they came to Jesus and saw that he was already dead, they did not break his legs. One of the soldiers thrust a lance into his side, and immediately blood and water flowed out.

(Jn 19:31-34)

- We adore you, O Christ, and we praise you.
- Because by your holy cross you have redeemed the world.

My Jesus, you concluded your earthly life. Under the cross your faithful Mother continued to suffer. Suffering had overcome her capacity for resistance. She could bear it no longer when she received your body on her knees, that body which she gave birth to in Bethlehem and looked after so well for so many years.

Message: Dear Children! I have already told you that I have chosen you in a special way, just as you are. I am the Mother that loves you all. In every instant, when you have difficulties, do not be afraid because I love you even when you are far away from me and my Son. I pray to you, do not let my heart weep with tears of blood for the souls who are lost in sin. Therefore, dear children, pray, pray, pray. Thank you for having responded to my call!

(24 May 1984)

- We thank you, O Mary, and we bless you.
- Because by your sufferings you helped to redeem the world.

O Mary, Mother of Sorrows, your breast was not icy with vendetta and hate but was warm and welcoming. It became that way from the pain which you suffered. You could warmly welcome the cold body of your martyr Son as you welcomed Him that day in Bethlehem. Now you offer Him to the Father for our salvation, like the time you presented Him at the temple, where you offered Him to the Father as your first born. You experienced the realization of the prophetic words of Simeon with infinite pain. He prophesized to you that a sword would pierce your motherly heart.

Thank you, O Mary, because you did not let yourself be frightened by the suffering and you did not run away. Thank you for your faith. I want to express to you, with my life and with my love, that I would like to console you and give you joy. So now, I consecrate myself to you and I put myself at your service, O Mary.

Gather all the Church under your protection, particularly in these difficult times. Welcome, O Mary, all men and allow them to be attracted by your love. Your maternal heart warms every heart that is frozen and struggling in sin. O Mary, may all those who sit on your motherly lap become brothers and sisters. By your intercession may peace run and flood all the earth like a large river. O Mary, be the mother of abandoned children and of all those who are rejected by their dear ones. Stop similar situations from occurring. O Mary, may it be that from your motherly breast are born holy families, where peace and love will reign. Amen!

Have mercy on us, O Lord!
Have mercy on us!

O Mary, Mother of Sorrows,
Intercede for us.

Christ, when You shall call me hence,
Be Your Mother my defense,
Be Your Cross my victory.

Holy Mother, pierce me through,
In my heart each wound renew,
Of my Savior crucified.

Ms. Alice J. Janny
7536 Cooper Point Rd NW
Olympia WA 98502

Jesus, your friends put you in the tomb

The cold and heavy structure of the tomb dominates the scene of the burial. Mary seems to light up the face of Jesus with a last embrace before He enters the darkness. It is the extreme act of the enormous sacrifice that is just about to be completed. In that sign of Mary's, is all the affection and tenderness that only a mother can express. All is wrapped in a climate of painful sorrow. The disciples cry at the entrance of the tomb while John observes the scene.

From the Bible: A grave was assigned him among the wicked and a burial place with evildoers, though he had done no wrong nor spoken any falsehood. But the Lord was pleased to crush him in infirmity. If he gives his life as an offering for sin, he shall see his descendants in a long life, and the will of the Lord shall be accomplished through him. Because of his affliction he shall see the light in fullness of days; through his suffering, my servant shall justify many, and their guilt he shall bear. Therefore, I will give him his portion among the great, and he shall divide the spoils with the mighty. Because he surrendered himself to death and was counted among the wicked; and he shall take away the sins of many, and win pardon for their offenses.

(Is 53:9-12)

- We adore you, O Christ, and we praise you.
- Because by your holy cross you have redeemed the world.

Jesus, they behaved inhumanely to you. The last act, that of the burial, is finally a humane and friendly act. Those who carry hate in their hearts, and those who persecute have gone. Around you we find Mary, your Mother, a few disciples and your beloved apostle John, with a few friends. Your Mother still has the strength to caress you and show you her great reverence.

O Jesus, with an act of love and of gratitude you are put in the tomb. The pain and emptiness are evident, but the hate has disappeared. Love is stronger, all is bearable.

Jesus, O my Lord, I pray to you now for all those who will die today in inhumane conditions, abandoned and rejected, alone; for those who will die on the roads because of accidents or in places of work, unexpectedly and suddenly. I pray particularly for those who kill and for their victims. Only you can light their faces, so that in them the last act will be the victory of love. I pray for the mothers, the fathers, and the doctors who kill innocent children. I pray to you also for those innocent victims, who even today undergo this sad end. Welcome them into your kingdom. They will have neither burial nor memory, but your love will mark them forever in the book of life.

FOURTEENTH STATION

Message: Dear Children! Today I invite you all to prayer. Without prayer, dear children, you are not able to experience God, nor me, nor the graces that I am giving you. Therefore, my call to you is that you always pray at the beginning and at the end of your day. Dear children, I desire to guide you, day by day, more and more in prayer. If you do not grow it will be because you do not desire it. I invite you, dear children, to make sure that prayer always  **takes first place. Thank you for having responded to my call!**

(3 July 1986)

- We thank you, O Mary, and we bless you.
- Because by your sufferings you helped to redeem the world.

O Mary, Mother of Jesus, in accompanying your Son, you found yourself in front of the tomb: I believe that the light of your face is illuminating the darkness of the tomb itself. Be close to those who today, in whatever way and whatever place, lift up their spirit to God. May your love illuminate the last moments of their lives, taking pain from their suffering. Your love will be an invitation to forgiveness and to reconciliation for those who treacherously and desperately kill others or take their own lives.

Have mercy on us, O Lord!
Have mercy on us!

O Mary, Mother of Sorrows,
Intercede for us.

While my body here decays,
May my soul Your goodness praise,
Safe in heaven eternally. Amen.

Holy Mother, pierce me through,
In my heart each wound renew,
Of my Savior crucified.

Jesus, you are gloriously resurrected from the dead

Three days after the resurrection! The strong stone boulder of the tomb is nearly crumbled by the radiant light that is shed from the risen Christ. Jesus appears suspended in mid-air in all his divinity and blazing, regal majesty. Nothing shows the terrible sufferings He experienced. It is He, the Messiah, the Son of God who returns with glory as He had promised! At His appearance the guards of the tomb are like victims of an explosion, they are thrown into confusion. All humanity is present in this impressive and conclusive scene and is represented by three witnesses. On the left, is a sleeping man. He is the "symbol" of those who are and remain indifferent to the mystery of the death and resurrection of Christ. On the right, is a terrified man who is covering his eyes. He doesn't want to see. He is the crushing failure of those who reject, with the resurrection, the transcendent immortality of Christ. At the center is one who opens himself to the light although it is already late.

Now The Virgin can adore her Son-God, in the glory of the Father.

FIFTEENTH STATION

From the Bible: On the evening of that first day of the week, even though the disciples had locked the doors of the place where they were for fear of the Jews, Jesus came and stood before them. "Peace be with you," he said. When he had said this, he showed them his hands and his side. At the sight of the Lord the disciples rejoiced.

(Jn 20:19-20)

- We adore you, O Christ, and we praise you.
- Because by your holy cross you have redeemed the world.

O Jesus, everything in your life would have been in vain if you had not risen. What would have remained of your words and your stories if you had not gloriously risen as you promised?

All would have disappeared like smoke in the wind. They would have dispersed like fog. But you are resurrected, O my Lord Jesus. Suffering has been transformed because of the resurrection. Death has been defeated. Hope has been healed. Love has received its deepest foundation and its motivation. Hate and hurt have been uncovered. A new reign is arriving; Yours O Jesus, a reign of resurrection and of thanks, of joy and of peace.

O resurrected Jesus, may your strong light penetrate us and disperse every darkness from our hearts, from families, from the Church and from the world so that in every place there will be, in harmony with you, a new song of joy and salvation. Allow each one of us to shout, "Alleluia" because you are alive and reigning. The tombs open and those that were spiritually dead receive new life. No one who has been guided by You will be excluded from the court of the resurrection.

Message: Dear Children! I would like to invite you to grow in love. A flower can not grow normally without water. So not even you, dear children, can grow without God's blessing. Everyday you must ask for His blessing to grow normally and to be able to fulfill your duties in union with God. Thank you for having responded to my call!

(10 April 1986)

- We thank you, O Mary, and we bless you.
- Because by your sufferings you helped to redeem the world.

O Mary, your joy is great, even greater than the amount that you had to suffer. You know how necessary the resurrection was for us. So, O Mother of the risen Lord, intercede so all of us can discover ourselves in the final joy of the resurrection.

Have mercy on us, O Lord!
Have mercy on us!

O Mary, Mother of Sorrows,
Intercede for us!

Queen of heaven, rejoice. Alleluia.
For He Whom you deserved to bear. Alleluia.
Has risen as He said. Alleluia. Pray for us to God. Alleluia.
Rejoice and be glad, O Virgin Mary. Alleluia.
For the Lord is truly risen. Alleluia.

Thank you, Jesus! Thank you, O Mary! I was able to reflect on the passion with which you, united in love, saved the world.

Thank you for the existential experience that brought me the resurrection so that everything can be transformed into good.

Thank you, because with new faith, with new joy and with renewed love, I can set out on the road to meet my fellow travelers, to soften human sufferings and anguish. Do not let me forget this experience. Make me a witness of the resurrection.

May the whole Church become a faithful witness to the resurrection before all men. Help everyone to become people of good will.

Amen. Alleluia!

THE CHAPLET OF THE SEVEN SORROWS
OF THE BLESSED VIRGIN MARY

We offer this chaplet to all those who, after having walked to Golgotha with Mary and Jesus, descend from Krizevac, or who, after praying the Way of The Cross at home or in Church, still have some time to meditate more deeply on the fullness of Our Lady's Sorrows. These sorrows are concentrated in the so called "Seven Sorrows," which have been the object of reflection and prayer in Marian devotion.

INTRODUCTORY PRAYER:

O dear Lady, Mother of Sorrows, I want to recall now all those moments in which you have suffered. After meditating on the mutual suffering with your Son, who remained in the grave, I want to remain with you and remember with deep gratitude all your grief.

I want to accompany you through your life of suffering while on this earth, and unite my sufferings with yours as well as with all the sufferings of mothers and fathers, of all sick young men and women, and of children and elderly people. May all sufferings be accepted with love and may all crosses be carried with hope. Amen!

FIRST SORROW OF MARY

Mary, you have presented your Son in the Temple and the aged Simeon, a holy man, announced to you that your first-born would become a symbol of opposition and that your soul would be pierced by a sword of pain. This was the first sword to pierce your soul. You have pondered this word like all the others. Thank you Mary. I am presenting this first sorrow for all parents who in many different ways suffer because of their children.

OUR FATHER ... 7 HAIL MARYS...

Blessed be the suffering of Mary, Our Mother!

SECOND SORROW OF MARY

Mary, it is difficult to imagine all the feelings that you had, when at the invitation of your spouse, you got up in the middle of the night to flee with your child, this child in whom you recognized and adored the Messiah, and the Son of God.

You were left without the securities that the homeland and the homely stove can offer. You fled, and so you associated yourself with those who have no roof above their heads and who live in foreign lands, without a homeland.

Mary, as a mother I pray to you for all those who have to leave their homes for whatever reason. I pray for all refugees and for all in exile; for all the poor who have not the means to build homes for their family.

Especially, I pray for those who, as a result of family conflict, have abandoned their family and are now living in the streets; for young people who do not agree with their parents; for the divorced, and for the rejected. Through their sufferings may you lead them to their new home.

OUR FATHER ... 7 HAIL MARYS...

Blessed be the suffering of Mary, Our Mother!

THIRD SORROW OF MARY

Mary, for three days you looked for your Son, in sadness. You found him happy in the Temple. Sadness lasted in your heart for a long time. Your torment was great because you were aware of your responsibility. The Father had entrusted you with His Son, the Messiah, the Savior. That is why your sadness was so great. After finding Jesus you were filled with joy.

O Mary, I pray to you now for the young who have drifted away from their family homes and are suffering because of it. I also pray for those who had to leave their homes because of sickness, and for all those who might be abandoned in hospitals. Especially I pray Mary, for all those young people who have not been given enough love and do not know what it means to have a family home. Search for them. Let them be found so that a new world will be possible.

OUR FATHER ... 7 HAIL MARYS...

Blessed be the suffering of Mary, Our Mother!

FOURTH SORROW OF MARY

Mary, you have met your Son while He was carrying the cross. Who could describe the pain you felt in that moment? I find myself without words... O Most Holy Mother, I pray for those who are left alone in their pain. Visit those in prison and comfort them. Visit the sick. Go to those who are lost. Bring a caress to those who are infected by an incurable disease, just as you caressed your Son for the last time on this earth. Help them to offer their sufferings for the salvation of the world just as you did at your Son's side.

OUR FATHER ... 7 HAIL MARYS...

Blessed be the suffering of Mary, Our Mother!

FIFTH SORROW OF MARY

Mary, you were standing under your Son's cross. You accompanied him in anguish and stood under the cross and that pain could not be consoled. Mary, your faith was great in your suffering. With courage you stood beneath the cross. Your pain did not close your heart to new responsibilities. Through your Son's wish you became the Mother of all of us.

Mary, I pray for all those who are close to those who are suffering. Help them so that they can nurse them with love. Encourage those who are exhausted because of caring for their sick ones. Especially bless all mothers with sick children. May their standing next to their crosses be their salvation. Unite with your motherly suffering the exhausting efforts of those who are called to care for their dear ones who are sick for long periods of time, or even for a lifetime.

OUR FATHER ... 7 HAIL MARYS...

Blessed be the suffering of Mary, Our Mother!

SIXTH SORROW OF MARY

With your grief filled soul you accept the lifeless body of your Son, holding Him upon your motherly lap. Your pain continues after He died, but still you hold Him close to your heart as if to warm Him.

Mary, I devote myself to you. I give you my pain and the pain of all people. I offer to you all the lonely, the deserted, the rejected and those in broken relations. I offer to you all the world. May all be held upon your motherly lap. May the world become your family, and all of us your brothers and sisters.

OUR FATHER ... 7 HAIL MARYS...

Blessed be the suffering of Mary, Our Mother!

SEVENTH SORROW OF MARY

Mary, you accompanied Jesus to His grave. You have sobbed and cried over Him like one cries for an only son. There are many sad people in the world today because they have lost their dear ones. Comfort those who seek comfort in the faith.

Many are without faith and hope, and they get lost in the problems of this world, losing hope and the joy of life. Mary, seek for them faith. May they find the right path. May all evil be destroyed, so that new life can spring forth just as it grew from your suffering and from your Son's grave.

OUR FATHER ... 7 HAIL MARYS...

Blessed be the suffering of Mary, Our Mother!

Ms. Alice J. Janny
7536 Cooper Point Rd NW
Olympia WA 98502